תֵּבַת נֹחַ

NOAH'S ARK

תֵּבַת נֹחַ

NOAH'S ARK

Adapted by
Alison Greengard

Illustrated by
Carol Racklin-Siegel

EXCERPTED FROM
THE BOOK OF GENESIS

EKS Publishing Co., Albany, California

For all my family in Israel.
—Alison

To my father, Louis Racklin, who loves
and encourages me in all I do.
—Carol

Adapted by
Alison Greengard

Illustrated by
Carol Racklin-Siegel

Editor
Jessica Goldstein

Book Design
Irene Imfeld

EKS Publishing Co.
P.O. Box 9750
Berkeley, CA 94709-0750
e-mail: orders@ekspublishing.com
Phone 1-877-743-2739
www.ekspublishing.com

First Printing, July 2003
ISBN 0-939144-00-0

Introduction

Noah's Ark continues the EKS Publishing series of Bible stories for young readers. The account of Noah and the great flood is told in Genesis 6-9, and although we have omitted words and sentences to keep the language simple and tighten the narrative, we have not changed or added any text. Each page offers a meaningful—but not always literal—translation. For readers studying Hebrew, we have included a literal translation at the end of the story. A glossary at the back of the book gives the meaning and pronunciation of each word in Noah's Ark. The glossary lists words exactly as they appear in the story.

The story of Noah is one of the best-known passages in Genesis. It is also a story that simultaneously demonstrates Israel's ties to and distinctiveness from other ancient Middle-Eastern civilizations. Many civilizations in the ancient world had flood stories. Israel's neighbors to the east told a story about gods bringing a flood because the noise of human life disturbed their peace. As in the story of Noah, one man survived the deluge. Also like the story of Noah, the gods repent and promise to never again destroy the earth.

What makes the Hebrew version unique is the reason given for the flood: It may be the first story to attribute the flood to the evilness of human beings. According to Genesis, God judges Noah alone to be righteous. Therefore, God decides that Noah and his family should survive the flood and be the ones to repopulate the earth after the waters recede. The story of the flood is about many things: It is about evil being destroyed, the righteous being saved, and the origin and symbolism of rainbows. You can also read the story of the flood as a second creation account or a story of re-creation. In Genesis 1-2, God creates light, heaven and earth, all animals, and human beings. Meanwhile, in Genesis 6-9, God brings devastation to the earth as a means to recreate it. Adam and Eve may have been the father and mother of humanity, but everyone living today descends more specifically from Noah and the three sons who survived him.

We hope that readers of all ages will enjoy this telling of Noah's Ark and come to appreciate the language and beauty of the Hebrew Bible.

נֹחַ אִישׁ צַדִּיק
אֶת הָאֱלֹהִים הִתְהַלֶּךְ נֹחַ.
וַתִּשָּׁחֵת הָאָרֶץ וַתִּמָּלֵא הָאָרֶץ חָמָס.

Noah was a good man,
and Noah walked with God.
But the earth was wicked
and full of violence.

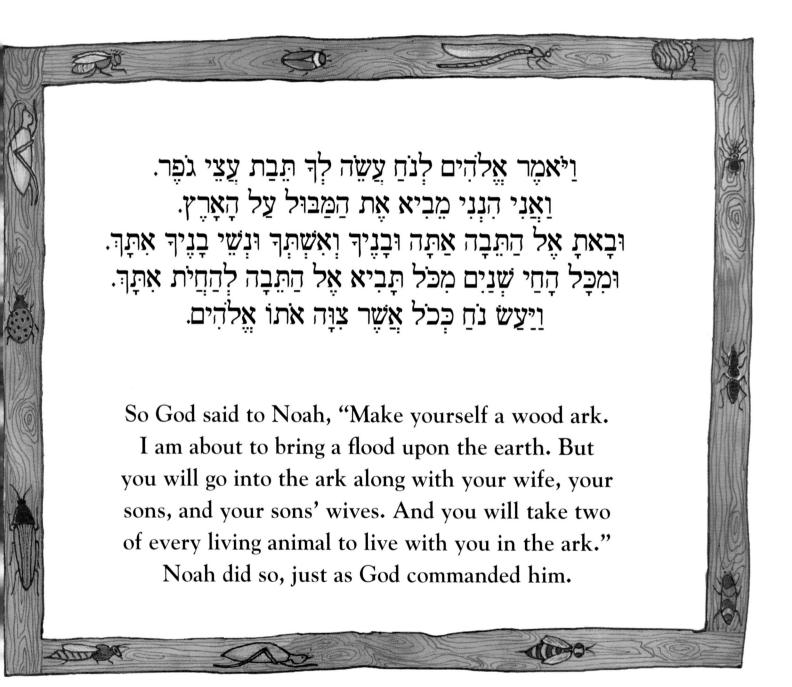

וַיֹּאמֶר אֱלֹהִים לְנֹחַ עֲשֵׂה לְךָ תֵּבַת עֲצֵי גֹפֶר.
וַאֲנִי הִנְנִי מֵבִיא אֶת הַמַּבּוּל עַל הָאָרֶץ.
וּבָאתָ אֶל הַתֵּבָה אַתָּה וּבָנֶיךָ וְאִשְׁתְּךָ וּנְשֵׁי בָנֶיךָ אִתָּךְ.
וּמִכָּל הָחַי שְׁנַיִם מִכֹּל תָּבִיא אֶל הַתֵּבָה לְהַחֲיֹת אִתָּךְ.
וַיַּעַשׂ נֹחַ כְּכֹל אֲשֶׁר צִוָּה אֹתוֹ אֱלֹהִים.

So God said to Noah, "Make yourself a wood ark.
I am about to bring a flood upon the earth. But
you will go into the ark along with your wife, your
sons, and your sons' wives. And you will take two
of every living animal to live with you in the ark."
Noah did so, just as God commanded him.

וַיְהִי הַגֶּשֶׁם עַל הָאָרֶץ
אַרְבָּעִים יוֹם וְאַרְבָּעִים לָיְלָה.
וַיִּרְבּוּ הַמַּיִם וַיְכַסּוּ כָּל הֶהָרִים.
וַיִּשָּׁאֶר אַךְ נֹחַ וַאֲשֶׁר אִתּוֹ בַּתֵּבָה.

The rain fell upon the earth for forty days
and forty nights. The water grew so deep that the
mountains were covered. Only Noah and those
that were with him in the ark were left.

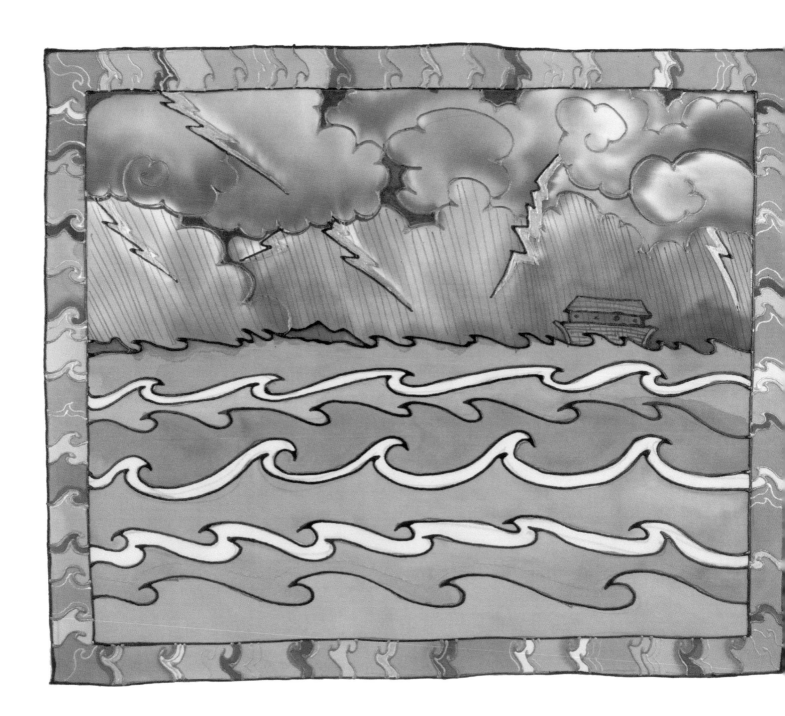

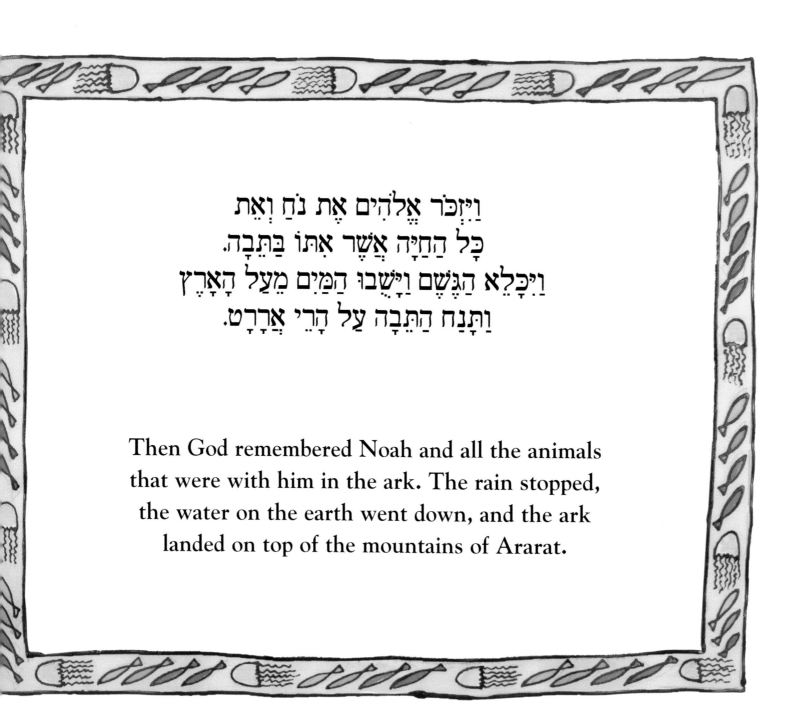

וַיִּזְכֹּר אֱלֹהִים אֶת נֹחַ וְאֵת
כָּל הַחַיָּה אֲשֶׁר אִתּוֹ בַּתֵּבָה.
וַיִּכָּלֵא הַגֶּשֶׁם וַיָּשֻׁבוּ הַמַּיִם מֵעַל הָאָרֶץ
וַתָּנַח הַתֵּבָה עַל הָרֵי אֲרָרָט.

Then God remembered Noah and all the animals
that were with him in the ark. The rain stopped,
the water on the earth went down, and the ark
landed on top of the mountains of Ararat.

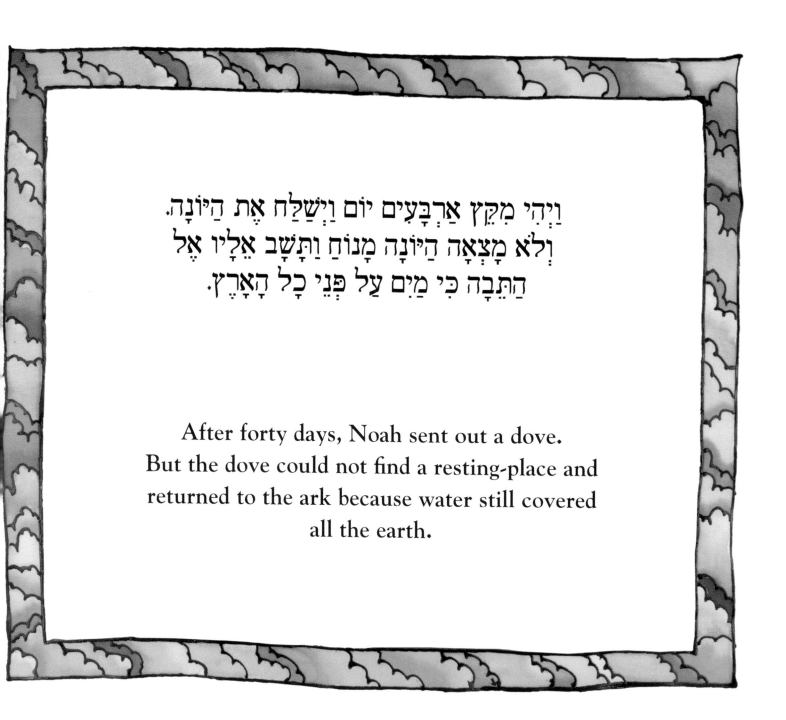

וַיְהִי מִקֵּץ אַרְבָּעִים יוֹם וַיְשַׁלַּח אֶת הַיּוֹנָה.
וְלֹא מָצְאָה הַיּוֹנָה מָנוֹחַ וַתָּשָׁב אֵלָיו אֶל
הַתֵּבָה כִּי מַיִם עַל פְּנֵי כָל הָאָרֶץ.

After forty days, Noah sent out a dove.
But the dove could not find a resting-place and
returned to the ark because water still covered
all the earth.

וַיָּחֶל עוֹד שִׁבְעַת יָמִים
אֲחֵרִים וַיֹּסֶף שַׁלַּח אֶת הַיּוֹנָה.
וַתָּבֹא אֵלָיו הַיּוֹנָה וְהִנֵּה עֲלֵה זַיִת בְּפִיהָ.
וַיֵּדַע נֹחַ כִּי קַלּוּ הַמַּיִם מֵעַל הָאָרֶץ.

Noah waited seven days, then sent out the dove
again. And when the dove came back, she had an
olive branch in her mouth! Now Noah knew that
the water on the earth had gone down.

וַיָּסַר נֹחַ אֶת מִכְסֵה הַתֵּבָה
וַיַּרְא וְהִנֵּה חָרְבוּ פְּנֵי הָאֲדָמָה.
וַיְדַבֵּר אֱלֹהִים אֶל נֹחַ לֵאמֹר צֵא מִן
הַתֵּבָה אַתָּה וְאִשְׁתְּךָ וּבָנֶיךָ וּנְשֵׁי בָנֶיךָ אִתָּךְ.
כָּל הַחַיָּה אֲשֶׁר אִתְּךָ הוֹצֵא אִתָּךְ.

Then Noah took the cover off the ark, looked out,
and saw dry land. And God said to Noah,
"Leave the ark, you along with your wife and your
sons and your sons' wives. And all the animals that
are with you, bring them out, too!"

וַיְבָרֶךְ אֱלֹהִים אֶת נֹחַ.
וַיֹּאמֶר אֱלֹהִים אֶל נֹחַ וַאֲנִי מֵקִים אֶת
בְּרִיתִי אִתְּכֶם וְלֹא יִהְיֶה עוֹד מַבּוּל לְשַׁחֵת הָאָרֶץ.
אֶת קַשְׁתִּי נָתַתִּי בֶּעָנָן וְהָיְתָה לְאוֹת
בְּרִית בֵּינִי וּבֵין הָאָרֶץ.

God blessed Noah. And God said to Noah,
"I promise you that a flood will never destroy
the earth again. I have put a rainbow
in the clouds, and it is a symbol of the bond
between me and the earth."

וַיִּהְיוּ בְנֵי נֹחַ הַיֹּצְאִים
מִן הַתֵּבָה שֵׁם וְחָם וָיָפֶת.
וּמֵאֵלֶּה נָפְצָה כָל הָאָרֶץ.

The sons of Noah who came out of the ark
were Shem, Ham, and Japheth, and the whole
world branched out from them.

19

Noah was a righteous man. Noah walked with God. But the earth became corrupt and was filled with violence.

God said to Noah, "Make yourself an ark from gopher wood, for behold, I am about to bring a flood upon the earth. But you will come into the ark: you, your sons, your wife, and your sons' wives with you. And of all the living animals, two of each you will bring to live with you in the ark." Noah did all that God commanded him.

There was rain on the earth for forty days and forty nights. The waters increased, and the mountains were covered. Only Noah and those that were with him in the ark were left.

Then God remembered Noah and all the animals that were with him in the ark. The rain was held back, the waters receded from the earth, and the ark came to rest on the mountains of Ararat.

At the end of forty days, Noah sent out the dove. But the dove cound not find a resting place and returned to him, to the ark, for the waters were still upon the face of the earth.

Noah waited seven days, then sent out the dove again. And when the dove came back to him—behold!—she had an olive branch in her mouth! Noah then knew that the waters had subsided on the earth.

Noah took the cover off the ark, and he looked out, and —behold!—there was dry land. Then God said to Noah, "Go out of the ark, you along with your wife and your sons and your sons' wives. And bring out with you all the animals that are with you."

God blessed Noah. And God said to Noah, "I make a covenant with you that there will never again be a flood to destroy the earth. I have set my bow in the clouds, and it will be a sign of the covenant between me and the earth." The sons of Noah who came out of the ark were Shem, Ham, and Japheth, and the whole earth branched out from them.

Glossary

א

אֲחֵרִים	a-chay-**reem**	more
אִישׁ	**eesh**	man
אַךְ	**ach**	only
אֶל	**el**	to
אֱלֹהִים	e-lo-**heem**	God
אֵלָיו	ay-**lav**	to him
אַרְבָּעִים	ar-ba-**eem**	forty
אֲרָרָט	a-ra-**rat**	Ararat
אֲשֶׁר	a-**sher**	that/which
אֶת	**et**	"with"
אֶת/אֵת	**et/ayt**	not translatable
אַתָּה	at-**ta**	you
אִתּוֹ	eet-**to**	with him
אֹתוֹ	ot-**to**	of him
אִתָּךְ	eet-**tach**	with you
אִתְּךָ	eet-te-**cha**	with you
אִתְּכֶם	eet-te-**chem**	with you

ב

בֵּינִי	bay-**nee**	between me
בְּנֵי	ve-**nay**	the sons of
בָּנֶיךָ	va-**ne**-cha	your sons
בֶּעָנָן	be-a-**nan**	in the clouds
בְּפִיהָ	be-**fee**-ha	in her mouth

22

אבגדהוזחטיכלמנסעפצקרשת

א
ב
ג
ד
ה
ו
ז
ח
ט
י
כ
ל
מ
נ
ס
ע
פ
צ
ק
ר
ש
ת

בְּרִית	be-**reet**	covenant
בְּרִיתִי	be-ree-**tee**	my covenant
בַּתֵּבָה	bat-tay-**va**	in the ark

ג

גֹפֶר	**go**-fer	gopher (wood)

ה

הָאֲדָמָה	ha-a-da-**ma**	the earth
הָאֱלֹהִים	ha-e-lo-**heem**	God
הָאָרֶץ	ha-**a**-rets	the earth
הַגֶּשֶׁם	ha-**ge**-shem	the rain
הֶהָרִים	he-ha-**reem**	the mountains
הוֹצֵא	hav-**tsay**	bring out
הַחַי	ha-**hai**	the living
הַחַיָּה	ha-chay-**ya**	the animals
הַיּוֹנָה	ha-yo-**na**	the dove
הַיֹּצְאִים	ha-yo-tse-**eem**	the ones who went out
הַמַּבּוּל	ha-mab-**bool**	the flood
הַמַּיִם	ha-**ma**-yeem	the waters
הִנְנִי	hee-ne-nee	behold (me)
הָרֵי	ha-**ray**	the mountains of
הַתֵּבָה	ha-tay-**va**	the ark
הִתְהַלֶּךְ	heet-hal-**lech**	he walked

ו

וַאֲנִי	va-a-**nee**	and I
וְאַרְבָּעִים	ve-ar-ba-**eem**	and forty

וַאֲשֶׁר	va-a-**sher**	and that/which
וְאִשְׁתְּךָ	ve-**eesh**-te-cha	and your wife
וְאֶת	ve-**ayt**	not translatable
וּבָאתָ	oo-**va**-ta	you will come
וּבֵין	oo-**vayn**	and between
וּבָנֶיךָ	oo-va-**ne**-cha	and your sons
וְהָיְתָה	ve-ha-ye-**ta**	and it will be
וְהִנֵּה	ve-**heen**-nay	and look!/behold!
וְחָם	ve-**cham**	and Ham
וַיֹּאמֶר	va-**yo**-mer	he said
וַיְבָרֶךְ	va-ye-va-**rech**	he blessed
וַיְדַבֵּר	va-ye-dab-**ber**	and he said
וַיֵּדַע	va-yay-**da**	and he knew
וַיְהִי	va-ye-**hee**	and there was
וַיִּהְיוּ	va-yeeh-**yoo**	it happened that
וַיִּזְכֹּר	va-yeez-**kor**	he remembered
וַיָּחֶל	va-ya-**chel**	he waited
וַיִּכְלָא	va-yeek-ka-**lay**	it stopped
וַיְכֻסּוּ	vay-choo-**soo**	they were covered
וַיֹּסֶף	va-**yo**-sef	again
וַיָּסַר	va-ya-sar	he took off
וַיַּעַשׂ	va-ya-**as**	he made/did
וְיֶפֶת	va-ya-**fet**	and Japheth
וַיַּרְא	va-**yar**	he looked out
וַיִּרְבּוּ	va-yeer-**boo**	they increased
וַיִּשָּׁאֶר	va-yeesh-sha-**er**	he was left

וַיָּשֻׁבוּ	va-ya-**shoo**-voo	they receded
וַיְשַׁלַּח	va-ye-shal-**lach**	he sent out
וְלֹא	ve-**lo**	and no/not
וּמֵאֵלֶּה	oo-may-ayl-**le**	and from them
וּמִכָּל	oo-meek-**kal**	and from all
וּנְשֵׁי	oo-ne-**shay**	and the wives of
וַתָּבֹא	vat-ta-**vo**	she came
וַתִּמָּלֵא	vat-teem-ma-**lay**	and it was filled
וַתָּנַח	vat-ta-**nach**	she came to rest
וַתָּשָׁב	vat-ta-**shav**	and she returned
וַתִּשָּׁחֵת	vat-teesh-sha-**chayt**	it became corrupt

ז

זַיִת	**za**-yeet	olive

ח

חָמָס	cha-**mas**	violence
חָרְבוּ	cha-re-**voo**	dried up

י

יִהְיֶה	yeeh-**ye**	it will be
יוֹם	**yom**	day/days
יָמִים	ya-**meem**	days

כ

כִּי	**kee**	for/because
כְּכָל	ke-**chol**	like/as all
כָּל\כָּל	**kol/chol**	all

לְאוֹת	le-**ot**	as a sign
לֵאמֹר	lay-**mor**	saying
לְהַחֲיֹת	le-ha-cha-**yot**	to live
לַיְלָה	**lai**-la	night/nights
לְךָ	le-**cha**	for yourself
לְנֹחַ	le-**no**-ach	to Noah
לְשַׁחֵת	le-sha-**chayt**	to destroy

מַבּוּל	mab-**bool**	flood
מֵבִיא	may-**vee**	I will bring
מַיִם	**ma**-yeem	water/waters
מִכֹּל	meek-**kol**	from all
מִכְסֶה	meech-**say**	cover
מִן	**meen**	from
מָנוֹחַ	ma-**no**-ach	resting place
מֵעַל	may-**al**	from
מָצְאָה	ma-tse-**a**	she found
מֵקִים	may-**keem**	(I) make
מִקֵּץ	meek-**kayts**	at the end of

נֹחַ	**no**-ach	Noah
נָפְצָה	na-fe-**tsa**	branched out
נָתַתִּי	na-tat-**tee**	I have put

 א
ב
ג
ד
ה
ו
ז
ח
ט
י
כ
ל
מ
נ
ס
ע
פ
צ
ק
ר
ש
ת

ע

עוֹד	**od**	still/yet/again
עַל	**al**	on
עָלֶה	a-**lay**	a branch of
עֲצֵי	a-**tsay**	wood of
עֲשֵׂה	a-**say**	you make

פ

פְּנֵי	pe-**nay**	the face of

צ

צֵא	**tsay**	go out
צַדִּיק	tsad-**deek**	righteous
צִוָּה	tseev-**va**	he commanded

ק

קַלּוּ	kal-**loo**	they subsided
קַשְׁתִּי	kash-**tee**	my bow

שׁ

שִׁבְעַת	sheev-**at**	seven
שָׁלַּח	shal-**lach**	he sent out
שֵׁם	**shaym**	Shem
שְׁנַיִם	she-**na**-yeem	two

ת

תָּבִיא	ta-**vee**	you will bring
תֵּבַת	tay-**vat**	ark of